BIG TOWNS,
BIG TALK

6/98

Enjoy!
I hope you find
inspiration here —

Patricia Smith

Patricia
Smith

BIG
TOWNS,
BIG
TALK

Z

ZOLAND BOOKS
Cambridge, Massachusetts

First edition published in 1992 by
Zoland Books, Inc.
384 Huron Avenue
Cambridge, Massachusetts 02138

Some of these poems have appeared in The Nation, Noctiluca,
TriQuarterly, The Paris Review, Agni, Red Brick Review, and Red Tree.

Grateful acknowledgment is made to Tia Chucha Press for permission to reprint the
following poems: "The Poetry Widow," "Sweet Daddy," and "Medusa." To
Warner/Chappell Music Co. for permission to quote from "Blues in the Night" by
Harold Arlen and Johnny Mercer. © 1941 Warner Bros. Inc. (Renewed). All rights
reserved.

FIRST EDITION

10 9 8 7 6 5 4 3 2

Printed in the USA by Braun Brumfield, Inc.; Ann Arbor, MI
Composition by Books International, Deatsville, AL
Book design by Boskydell Studio

Library of Congress Cataloging-in-Publication Data

Smith, Patricia, 1955-
    Big towns, big talk / Patricia Smith. — 1st ed.
      p.   cm.
    ISBN 0-944072-24-0 (pbk.) : $9.95
      1. Afro-American women—Poetry.   2. Social problems—Poetry.
    1. Title.
PS3569.M537839B5   1992   92-53829
811'.54—dc20   CIP

CONTENTS

I.

MY MAMA DONE TOLD ME . . .

Annie Pearl Smith Discovers Moonlight

My mother, the sage of Aliceville, Alabama,
didn't believe that men had landed on the moon.
"They can do anything with cameras,"
she hissed to anyone and everyone who'd listen,
even as moonrock crackled
beneath Neil Armstrong's puffed boot.
While the gritty film spun and rewound and we
heard the snarled static of "One small step,"
my mother pouted and sniffed
and slammed skillets into the sink.
She was not impressed.
After all, it was 1969, a year fat with deceit.
So many miracles
had proven mere staging for lesser dramas.

But why this elaborate prank
staged in a desert "somewhere out west,"
where she insisted the cosmic gag unfolded?
"They are trying to fool us."
No one argued, since she seemed near tears,
remembering the nervy deceptions of her own skin—
mirrors that swallowed too much,
men who blessed her with touch only as warning.
A woman reduced to juices, sensation and ritual,
my mother saw the stars only as signals for sleep.
She had already been promised the moon.

And heaven too. Somewhere above her head
she imagined bubble-cheeked cherubs
lining the one and only road to salvation,
angels with porcelain faces and celestial choirs
wailing gospel brown enough to warp the seams of paradise.
But for heaven to be real, it could not be kissed,
explored,
strolled upon
or crumbled in the hands of living men.
It could not be the 10 o'clock news,
the story above the fold,
the breathless garble of a radio "special report."

My mother had twisted her tired body into prayerful knots,
worked twenty years in a candy factory,
dipping wrinkled hands into vats of lumpy chocolate,
and counted out dollars with her thin, doubled vision,
so that a heavenly seat would be plumped for her coming.
Now the moon,
the promised land's brightest bauble,
crunched plainer than sidewalk beneath ordinary feet.
And her Lord just lettin' it happen.

"Ain't nobody mentioned God in all this," she muttered
over a hurried dinner of steamed collards and cornbread.
"That's how I know they ain't up there.
Them stars, them planets ain't ours to mess with.
The Lord woulda showed Hisself if them men
done punched a hole in my heaven."
Daddy kicked my foot beneath the table;

we nodded, we chewed, we swallowed.
Inside me, thrill unraveled;
I imagined my foot touching down on the jagged rock,
blessings moving like white light through my veins.

Annie Pearl Smith rose from sleep that night
and tilted her face full toward a violated paradise.
My father told me how she whispered in tongues,
how she ached for a sign
she wouldn't have to die to believe.

Now I watch her clicking like a clock toward deliverance,
and I tell her that heaven still glows wide and righteous
with a place waiting just for her,
fashioned long ago by that lumbering dance
of feet both human and holy.

Trying On Wedding Gowns
in Filene's Basement

Later, I laughed with my husband about the crowds,
the proper dames with their studied Boston curves,
hissing at price tags and leading with their nails.
Flustered mothers fluffed and swirled thick silk,
while their daughters compared diamonds. "Nothing
on the rack over $200, my gawd they're practically
giving them away. Honey hold your stomach in.
It's the only one left in your size. Just get married
in it, you can breathe later." Feeling smug and domestic,
I flashed my wife face at a pimpled coed crammed
into a silk sheath. Something in me ached to twinkle.

I was married in gold that winked when I walked,
a dress that once moved slowly through another man's
fingers. Innocent fabrics are wrong against my skin.
My soon-to-be husband, caged in
unaccustomed collar, held his breath, his eyes shining with ritual,
his feet folded into black shoes. There was no part of
him I didn't want freed, no skin I didn't want rubbed
raw, but the ceremony called for touch only twice.
The gold dress grew nervy, moved even when I didn't.

My mother's best friend snapped pictures neither my
husband or I have seen since. Our faces,
dark and bloated in Polaroid, seemed only slightly married.
I had a diamond, but nothing perfumed and precise,

nothing with angels. Real brides, I knew, choke on their love,
have their faces scrubbed clean, wonder why words
feel plump in their mouths. Even pulse inspires them.
The gold dress branded me pretender. Damn Barbie and
her stiff, snowy lace, her veiled inscrutable eyes.

I laughed with my husband about June brides gunning
for the ultimate bargain. But I didn't tell him
about the dresses I tried on. Pulling hard at faux pearls
and golden zippers, I felt old, sneaky, slippery as glass.
The first dress, gasping chiffon, flopped at my shoulders.
Buttons carved like fists slid from their openings,
and a flash of lacy black bra changed the room's geography.

I reached for my sequinned second choice, an explosion
of ivory light and thin netting, and stepped into its
monstrous weight. Sweeping the train 'round front,
I pulled myself to full primp in the mirror and waited for
a cacophony of bells, rose petals at the toes of my gym shoes.

Instead, I imagined my husband's beautiful hands at my neck
popping the first button, then—Barbie be damned—the second.

If I Cannot Dance

MARKETPLACE, TANGIER, 1990

"Sweet baby, brown baby, you want to buy?"

Men in shimmering cottons,
weaves of lemon and coral, purple and ash,
hair locked in dusty corkscrews,
flash gold from their grins as I pass.
The trinkets cradled in their palms
are worthless, grim little nuggets
with no holes for string or hooks for ears.
These men want pieces of my dollars,
a glimpse of thick Chicago in my hip.
But it is not their baubles I crave;
it is the skin of these sweet screamers,
the grimy black arc beneath each fingernail,
their stinging perfumes.
I want to open my mouth
upon the burnished swell of their forearms,
because I am brown baby, crazy American
with little time. The dust of Tangiers has
settled on my ankles, and I will go mad,
will sing to the moon, if I cannot dance.

These men think nothing of moving close,
brush the underside of my breast
with their offerings—faceless dolls with their
heads wrapped in tiny gasps of color,
wallets of tough hide, vials of animal scent.
One with an eye like pearl
pulls a shred from a hot, flat circle of bread,
pushes it into my mouth with his thumb,
laughs like a woman
when I bend to breathe in the steaming.
Fingers knot scarlet silk into my hair,
touch the oil of spices to the dip in my throat,
fold my toes in straw sandals.
"You want to buy?" breath full and sour on my cheek,
and I flip my muslin skirt, toss quarters
in the air, chew pungent chunks of mutton.

This is my first Africa. I will dance
with these dark men until my pockets are empty,
until my hair grows weak with their pulling,
until the moon wakes and demands my song.
"You want to buy?" Yes, yes, everything.
My nostrils widen and quiver, and home
is at the end of a million brown rivers.

Dylan, Two Days

for DYLAN CORBETT

The folks downstairs brought him home
yesterday, and I envied him his
discoveries—the warm certainty of milk,
the red-cheeked daddy, the anxious Labrador
sniffing the cradle's lace border.
Then there was the hungry way
his new eyes sifted light,
blinding him to borders,
and color slowly filling his ears,
every sound careening through thin bones.
In the middle of the day, while ice
gripped the windows and
my own son counted chest hairs,
I heard a tiny squall,
a roar riding on a breath string,
which I knew meant *"Where did my toes go?"*

Last night, Dylan slept,
curling into familiar circle,
stinging the air with his fists.
He dreamed of what he knew—
his mother's belly,
the harbor of her breathing.
In the bedroom above, my husband and I

made love, his teeth dragging along my spine,
sweat in my hair, my mouth opening to
pull him in. The bed buckled and banged
the wall. I screamed, almost into my pillow.
I remembered the new baby downstairs.

Maybe Dylan jumped,
maybe something ran through his sleeping,
maybe a pink finger found the sucking mouth.
I hope he wondered for a moment
at the strange, faraway rumble
before his body shivered still again,
since I have thought of no better way
to welcome him home.

Doctor Feelgood

Even the oldest women, knowing and toothless
in their porch rockers, don't remember the man
ever owning a name. But they can look at a
young girl, cracked like a branch across her
tousled bed, and they can smell the fever in her,
they can cluck low in their throats and wipe
her glittering brow with cool towels,
they can work their roots, pray and moan mojos
over the broken woman until the eldest among them
whispers, *"She gon die if we don't call him."*

Nobody knows his name.
But it is the angle of the moon that births him,
the low animal sound a woman makes when her
heart aches and swells toward bursting.
He hears and begins walking from wherever he is,
walking for miles through city streets
washed in their terrible light,
walking as the country crunches beneath his hard boots,
walking as sure as the night brings trouble,
his ears intent on the thick, bending wail of heartbreak.

He wades brown rivers,
struggles against the flat faces of mountains,
his traveling blues off-key and furious,
sung out to the woman who shrivels in a wooden bed,
wrapped in sheets bleached blue and bitter,

the fever eating her alive,
her heart twisted and cramped in its shrinking pocket.

Lady Day had a name for him. He cut through her blood
like the watery fire that bruised her throat beyond music.
She called him "Lover man," "Brown sugar," "Sweet papa."
Janis had a name for him. The blues that grated against
the back of her teeth screamed for his blessings
until blackness closed over the body she'd built
with her many fists. Aretha found his name, bringing it up
from her hips, where all such wisdom comes from.
She called him
Lee Cross,
Do Right Man,
Doctor *Feel*good.

Remember when he moved his hands across your hurting?

It is morning when the old women gather at the window
breathing beneath their patchwork, see him striding
through widening circles of sun, hear his foot fall
heavy on the porch. "The man here," one says. She says it
like *amen* at the end of a prayer, and the feverish girl
forces her eyes open against his light. He places one hand
on her head while the other hand moves across and into
the valleys women create with their pain,
every one of his fingers an open mouth,
his mouth a beautiful confusion of fingers,
slowly and patiently sealing each of the places
that ordinary men pry open again and again
with vows they believe to be real.

That Third Drink

He was that third drink she shouldn't have had,
a hammer moving down hard on her eyes.
He was the way fragrance moves in an empty room,
the hard stone that wouldn't stop prying at her closed eyes,
breaking her slumber into questions.
He was cyanide glistening in a china blue cup.
He was the pin prick hurting
that stiffens the hands after bullets of rain.

He was the bitch of moons, bright with disdain,
the sky's stuttering at twilight,
the nasty way neon winks at the lonely.

And she saw him clearly,
studied the lines of his face,
as she tumbled like an eager dancer
into the cave of his arms.
He was that third drink. She should have said no.

Now each time she grows thirsty,
he watches.

Dolls

he be ken and she be barbie
they house be concrete and glass
and her purse tells a circus story
and used to be full of cookies

mama say girl why your knees so rusty
but that baby smile and spit on her hand
and polish her skin back to brown
'cause she be barbie
and she can do anything
thought about putting food color
in her eyes
to make them blue

he be ken and she be barbie
she pulled his hand and made him play
don't wanna be nobody's man or have
no kids or play with no crazy girl just
wanna play ball
don't know what a daddy s'posed to do no way

she said be ken and he stood taller
then dropped to the ground with her
and made play babies with sticks

now you be ken, i'll be barbie
ain't nothing changed but time

we still make mirrors out of dirty water
and use that same water
to polish our knees
and if we gaze into that water long enough
damned if our eyes ain't blue

i know you would still rather play ball
but baby the game is over

Changing Partners

When Sam Cooke crooned "Bring Your Sweet Loving
On Home to Me," you could wrap your hips around that asking.
Wouldn't be no problem for my mama—
back in those days when she could—
to slip her body into that cool wail,
hiking up a skirt tight as a hiccup,
hypnotizing a row of whisky-soaked old men who only
wanted to squeeze *something* before closing time.
Or I can see her and my daddy,
tentative as matchsticks,
locked into one of those spine-twisting dips
with his nose nuzzling her throat,
searching for a basement, red-light rhythm to rule their lives.

But the first time I actually *saw* my mama dance,
her partner grabbed her heels and shook her till
she coughed music. His hands rubbed her skin raw
as he whipped her body through improbable spins,
snapping her back to him with a pop that startled her bones.
Runs roared through her stockings like rush-hour traffic,
swollen feet screamed in slingback pumps,
eyeglasses cracked in the chaos.
She pushed at him to calm the whirling,
but he hooked her wrists and held them,
twirled her into a twist
that slapped a howl from her throat.

The dancers stepped double-time until the walls sighed
and buckled around them, until the floor groaned with
mama's every frightened stomp, until everyone in the room
formed a circle with their bodies and circles with their mouths,
watching her arc through moves she shouldn't have survived.
Her eyes widened as the music braced for the bridge
and her partner's name grew large in her mouth,
the music no one else could hear grew sluggish and sexy and
the man no one could see coaxed a final bone-clanging shimmy.
Then he was done with her. Her body broke like a fever.

Mama tells me I'll dance too.
So I wait for the dancehall Jesus to move through me,
to fill me with hoseannas, rock me with hallelujahs,
to shake these bored bones.
I wait until the house lights slam on,
until greasy rags slide across the bartop,
until the music slurs to a stop.
I wait for the holy ghost to pull me out
onto the dance floor, whisper come-ons in my ear,
make me kick my heels above my head.

Mama says he'll come when I'm at peace.
But I'm what she was at 20, winking sleek,
moving only when there's a nasty mix, blue lights,
and a flesh-and-blood partner to press it all against.

Mr. Right, busy administering to the righteous,
keeps passing this place by,
sickened by the thick smoke, the cheap suits,
suspicious of my intentions.

After last call, they all wear the faces of saviors.
And I'm so tired of changing partners.

Speaking Out the Stars

for MICHAEL *and* BROTHER BLUE

Did you speak out the stars? Is that your song?
The twist of twilight from its glory orange heat
to whisper colors—was that your work?
It must have been your fingers that coaxed
the stubborn skin of morning to this softness.
Were you the father of this midnight, did you
pull me into this cradle of bunched starlight
and hold me there, weaving the sleepy color brown,
the color of my face, my knees, my hair,
into the patchwork of passage, into the jumbled quilt
of days that can no longer be reached for, or touched?

When my body stutters and I cry hallelujah
into the moon's many mouths, is that you crafting
those syllables of steam? Beneath your gentle mercies
I am convinced that Jesus breathes his shaking
into simple things—wood, candles, a toddling child.
And I know now that the stars—mystified by their
own unbridled fire, already drunk with blazing—
sprang from your throat. You knew how often
I would gaze upon their shifting light, how my eyes
would choke on their bright singing, how they would
pulse with glowing even after the both of us are gone.

Blonde White Women

They choke cities like snowstorms.

On the morning train, I flip through my *Ebony*,
marveling at the bargain basement prices
for reams of straightened hair
and bleaches for the skin. Next to me,
skinny pink fingers rest upon a briefcase,
shiver a bit under my scrutiny.
Leaving the tunnel, we hurtle into hurting sun.
An icy brush paints the buildings
with shine, fat spirals of snow
become blankets, and Boston stops breathing.

It is my habit to count them. So I search
the damp, chilled length of the train car
and look for their candle flames of hair,
the circles of blood at their cheeks,
that curt dismissing glare
reserved for the common, the wrinkled, the black.

I remember striving for that breathlessness,
toddling my five-year-old black butt around
with a dull gray mophead covering my
nappy hair, wishing myself golden.
Pressing down hard with my
carnation pink crayola, I filled faces
in coloring books, rubbed the waxy stick
across the back of my hand until the skin broke.

When my mop hair became an annoyance
to my mother, who always seemed to be mopping,
I hid beneath my father's white shirt,
the sleeves hanging down on either side of my head,
the coolest white light pigtails.
I practiced kissing, because to be blonde and white
meant to be kissed, and my fat lips slimmed
around words like "delightful" and "darling."
I hurt myself with my own beauty.

When I was white, my name was Donna.
My teeth were perfect; I was always out of breath.

In first grade, my blonde teacher
hugged me to her because I was the first
in my class to read, and I thought the rush
would kill me. I wanted her to swallow
me, to be my mother, to be the first fire
moving in my breast. But when she pried
me away, her cool blue eyes shining with
righteousness and too much touch,
I saw how much she wanted to wash.

She was not my mother,
the singing Alabama woman
who shook me to sleep
and fed me from her fingers.
I could not have been blacker
than I was at that moment.
My name is Patricia Ann.

Even crayons fail me now—
I can find no color darker,
more beautiful, than I am.
This train car grows tense with me.
I pulse, steady my eyes,
shake the snow from my short black hair,
and suddenly I am surrounded by snarling madonnas

demanding that I explain
my treachery.

Heartland

From a tiny black and white television
in a sullen truck stop just east of Advance, Ind.,
a sports announcer screams his voice to a squeak.
Mike Andretti, six laps away from winning at Indy,
has pulled his machine over smoothly, without sputter,
without benefit for a final dramatic choking.
The announcer is clearly insulted by this affront
to American values, and is trying very hard
to remain objective, trying hard not to yell
"Get back on the road, you chickenshit sonofabitch!"

I tune out his feverish buzz and glance at the four
proprietors of this gastronomic hellhole—
the pimply, slack-jawed son swiping at chipped dishes
with an oily rag, his sister the waitress with eyes
Maybellined into a jolting blackness and her
front teeth smoked away, grandma fingering blue–rinsed
hair and gnawing on something invisible,
and the beehived gumcracker in charge, smelling
very much like gingham, mothballs and Advance, Ind.

All four have swiveled on the creaking stools
to stare at me, all of me much blacker than they
can imagine, much more of a show than the tiny
cars whizzing around the screen, much more shocking
than Mike Andretti's white light moment of failure.

If it were summer, fat flies, drunk on bacon grease,
would drag their last across this tabletop. As it is,
I am sitting across from my white husband, and we are
hungry, angry, and for the moment, strangers.
I refuse to eat and amuse myself instead by watching
the Waltons try to figure us out—me sipping
vehemently on lukewarm Diet Pepsi, my husband inhaling
three mutant pieces of country-fried chicken.

He picked that colored girl up at the race, and now
he regrets it. He's a pimp from Ohio, a businessman
who picks up hitchers. She fucks him for money.
She twists her body the way he wants it, for money.
They all agree I'm in it for the cash,
that he's in it for whatever that song is
black women sing with their bodies. They're all wrong.

I wonder if my husband really understands how I feel
in places like this, beneath eyes like these,
right in the path of the hiss, "She fucks him for money."
He studied with Robert Hayden, taught at the blackest
college in one of America's blackest cities,
understands glass ceilings and the politics of black rage,
but has he ever worn his bones on the outside?
Has he ever walked into a room of drained faces
and felt the lights dim, the ventilation choke?
I love his thick hands, the way he rejoices that there
is no skin other than mine. He loves my mouth, that moves
across his map the way I'd moved across this country,
never stopping to think that it might not be mine.

Elk City, Oklahoma. Kickapoo State Park. Carlin, Nevada.
Morro Bay, California. Lynch Road in Danville, Illinois.
Paducah, Kentucky. Grant, Colorado. Boston, Massachusetts.
A truck stop in Advance, Indiana.

This is not my heartland.
However, this *is* my heart, pumping hard through
ribbons of cornfields and sleek shopping centers;
this is my heart, stopping whenever we walk
into a restaurant and clocks slam shut;
this is my heart
throbbing wild in those dim convenience stores
that sell hats embroidered with shotguns,
Confederate flag belt buckles and earrings,
stale cupcakes with bright pink frosting
and those cheap goddamned souvenirs you shake
to see fat flakes of white snow
fall on any one of a million American cities.

But Only Eye

i'm of that peculiar 3 a.m. mindset,
all thighs, wavering morale. i clamp
down on words that threatened to escape
into air i breathe by myself.
ashamed of my hips, so frightened of singing.

i imagine you sleeping, turning toward
your window, peeling me precisely
from your dreams. under too many blankets,
your only nasty nocturnal habit.
boom. again a star shrieks, scarring
the sky with its voice. but only i see.
my lips so full,
my hair refusing to sit still.

if you were not you, what would
i do with my mouth? how many mornings
like this, moonwashed, your face in my fingers,
those fingers warming me like whiskey?
it doesn't take long with your fire
nipping at me. boom. again a star wails blue.
but only i see.

i think of your skin, too warm,
scented deep like wood,
beneath too many tangled blankets. boom.

i send out a cry, my belly straining for the stars.
but only i see. and you, longing

to be master of this 3 a.m. drama, miss
everything, miss nothing. boom. again
the sun gives up as i lie back and
wait for your sighs, those potent little fucks,
to reach me, boom. on the night wind.

What I Didn't Learn

Determined not to write a poem glorifying loss,
I work you into paper using my fingers.
Isolated facts rise to glow on the nubby surface.

On Wednesday, the 17th of June, we held hands
and crossed a wide street. Our bodies were
uneasy with wanting, our words fists and roses.

We stretched those bodies beneath trees. Each movement
we made was discussed, each heat carefully dissected.
A moan waited nearby. Buildings fell upon our voices
as we made love like clumsy thieves,
itching wildly through interruptions in our clothes.

Then, the walking alone, the flattened perspective.
I hear it's all done with mirrors.
Phone bells with no voices there
and my fingers rubbing lies onto paper.

Shaving

The man who makes my body stutter wears a beard to hide his face.
But I've seen the pictures—in them,
his chin struggles toward square,
certain but imperfect. Black-rimmed glasses rest upon an
unfamiliar nose. No questions cramp the space above his eyes.
He had the world by the balls and knew it. Or at least he knew
that the world had balls, and approximately where they were.
I can imagine him clutching a shot glass of something bitter,
nuzzling a perfect ear, laughing from a place too deep to touch.
Somewhere in Chicago, I am struggling with chemistry,
teetering on platform shoes, not yet old enough to confuse him.

The man who touches an uneven lip to my face
believes that the only faults that matter are hidden
beneath that rough wiry explosion on his cheeks and chin.
I want his skin shaved clean, I want to see flecks
of fresh blood. I want to rip the hair away with my teeth.
Instead, I hold his limp, veined penis in my hand
and watch it move against my fingers, growing the way
a new word grows in a child's mouth. I search for new places
to take him in, new walls to tighten against his moving,
new sounds to bring to his throat. He does not hear
my whispered "michael," the "m" gripping the air like steam,
as he straddles me and all his faces
fall to shatter against my neck.

The man who says "I *need*" like he is gasping for breath
believes I will never see his true face, that I will never
know the man who stood dazed as wives crumbled around him,
the laughing bear who tumbled four small sons in his lap.
Now he reads me poems, breathes into my open mouth,
slips questions into my waiting body. I bury my fingers
in his beard, tug a little, wonder what bright scars I would find.
I am obsessed with razors, with fat lather bursting spice smell.
He stares at me with a trust no one deserves.

He does not know what I see when he throws his head back
in the night, when he chokes on sweat and spit and
fills my nose, my hair, with what he has held inside.
The face I imagine then is smooth, bare, white,
and the circle of his mouth sputters moonlight.

I want to be all that he ever loves,
and now that he is my teacher
I will show him what I have learned. Patience.
I move my mouth across his face, spit out a hair.

The Poetry Widow

You've known me long enough to know
that my longings are sometimes without reason.

Tonight, I wished I was one of your poems,
strong syllables curled in your throat
awaiting a joyous delivery. I wished
I was that clever, stilted script on
the paper in your hand, words you sweat over.

I wanted to feel your thick hands move over me,
urging my spirit from the page. Tonight, as I
crawled into old music and warm, scented water,
as I filled myself with the steamed onions and rice
you'd left for me, as I wondered aloud
about the hole in the middle of the room where I stood,

I wished I was one of your poems. I wanted to be
a strong movement in your mouth, a shock to your audience.
I wanted your first and last word to be me. I needed applause.

The Lord Works Silvio's

Thirty years ago, my mother stopped wearing slacks.
Locked into the twine time at Silvio's on Lake Street,
she suddenly felt the devil at work
in her squat brown legs.
Willie James, my daddy's best friend
only when my daddy was around,
was swinging my mama damned near over his head,
Tyrone Davis singing baby won't you change your mind
and she almost had, that little bit of JB
had found her ankles and clicked them loose,
with nosy Miss Sarah James
watching from her ringside table:
"That Annie Pearl Smith don't back up off my man,
I'll cut her throat so bad
that phony gold necklace won't have no place to sit."
Sarah James gulping that firewater like it's
oxygen, and talking long, lean lines of shit.

Meanwhile, my mama wondered
who put the batteries in her toes.
She wanted to rip the slacks from her legs,
she wanted to go crazy in love, to leave the wild arc
of her fingernail in someone's skin.
She wanted cool, fluid fingers
to spin her in an endless bop,
a faceless dance where she moved like hot sauce,

a dance that went on forever
so she'd never grow too old to remember
the words to the songs they played in dark places.

Her legs felt like drums. The cheap slacks
bit into her and only the rhythm line changed
as she fastened another dance partner
onto the ends of her arms while
Willie slid back to his wife, that one gold tooth
sparkling my mama's way,
flashing that secret sign
that made women turn to Jesus and back again.

When the scream moved through her, the sound
bounced like a bullet off the walls
and that high thin cry was the night's first perfect music,
it was the sound and the dance to the sound,
it was the peculiar music
of a woman needing to free those guilty legs
that had moved far beyond her,
tangled in the nastiest rhythm she knew,
and religion was the only way out.

That Friday night, at Silvio's on Lake Street,
my mother offered herself to God.
He was her final partner,
sliding her roughly across the floor to the door,
finally freeing her sweaty satin legs
to walk the straight,
to walk the narrow.

II.

BIG TOWNS, BIG TALK

Doin' the Louvre

PARIS, DECEMBER 1991

for PATRICIA ZAMORA

You're a junkie just like I am.

After we dump your husband in the Louvre's cafe
to sip the steaming tea and chew on his poetry,
we're off like schoolgirls, screeching in duet,
dazzled by the bright eternal gasp of ancient things.

We've got no business here, homegirl and *compañera,*
we've got no business
working our mouths around his sharp, exquisite language
or savoring the sweet-tongue squeeze of pastries,
shining cakes and shaved chocolate.

We're of simpler stock—city and country dust,
collard greens, salsa picante, hopscotch,
moonpies, bulletholes and basement slow dances.
We are shamelessly American,
rough street girls with rusty knees,
the flip side of cocky Parisian wisps
in slim cashmere coats the color of tobacco.

Girlfriend, you and I are too much scream for this place,
but you're a junkie just like I am.

Too long denied access to official beauty,
we walk these streets
with our mouths open and faces tilted up,
swallowing everything, swallowing it all,
much too much scenery and sound
for our thin American throats.
We gawk at cathedrals with their gargoyles
bleached to an eerie snarl
by bright slashes of moon,
say *goodbye* when we mean *yes,*
good morning when we mean *how much,*
ask for bread when we need the toilet.
We are amazed that no one is asking for all of this back,
that we are allowed to bask in this city's light.

I can still hear my mother,
as plain and practical as a cast iron skillet:
"You need to stop all that foolishness
over there in some France
where you don't know nothing or nobody.
Ain't no black folks over there no way."

But I know you, old friend,
with your burnished tangle of hair
and deep laugh,
and right now these halls belong to us.
There are
bad
girls
loose

in the Louvre,
girls soft as gunshots,
girls nourished and fueled by silvers, silks,
and the stone gaze of Napoleon.

We laugh at the smashed noses of Egyptian rulers,
stare at the tiny mummified feet of a young girl,
mistake Goya for Gauguin
and rub what surfaces we can,
including the marble cocks of towering deities.
When we say things like,
"Hey, I think I saw this one on a postcard once,"
or, "Do you know how old this thing is?"
how can the world help but love us?
We would give Venus our arms.

After seven hours
clicking our hungry heels
and snapping illicit flash photos
in dark halls brimming with whispered music,
we find the Mona Lisa alone,
caged and antiseptic
behind the glass every woman wears,
and we wonder how best to free her,
knowing she's a junkie just like we are.

She longs for our wild voices,
our naive, accidental beauty.
She's achin' to ditch that frame

and skip these hallowed halls with the homegirls,
mistake the obscene for the exquisite,
and gaze at unsolved mysteries
that just for once
are not her own.

Biting Back

Children do not grow up
as much as they grow away.
My son's eyes are stones—flat, brown, fireless,
with no visible openings in or out.
His voice, when he cares to try it on,
hovers one-note in that killing place
where even the blues fidget.
Tight syllables, half-spoken, half-spat,
greet me with the warmth
of glint-tipped arrows. The air around him
hurts my chest, grows too cold to nourish,
and he stares past me to the open door of his room,
anxious for my trademark stumbled retreat.

My fingers used to brush bits of the world
from his kinked hair,
but he has moved beyond that mother shine
to whispered "fucks" on the telephone,
to the sweet mysteries of pearl buttons
dotting the maps of young girls,
to the warped, frustrating truths of algebra,
to anything but me. Ancient, annoying apparatus,
I have retained the ability to warm meat,
to open cans, to clean clothing
that has yellowed and stiffened.
I spit money when squeezed,

don't try to dance in front of his friends,
and know that rap music cannot be stopped.
For these brief flashes of cool, I am tolerated in spurts.

At night, I lie in my husband's arms
and he tells me that these are things that happen,
that the world will tilt right again
and our son will return, unannounced, as he was—
goofy and clinging, clever with words, stupefied by rockets.
And I dream on that.
One summer after camp,
12 inches taller than the summer before,
my child grinned and said,
"Maybe a tree bit me."

We laughed,
not knowing that was to be his last uttered innocence.
Only months later, eyes narrowed and doors slammed.
Now he is scowls, facial hair, knots of muscle. He is
pimp, homey, pistol. He is man smell, grimy fingers,
red eyes, rolling dice. He is street, smoke, cocked cannon.

I sit on his bare mattress after he's left for school,
wonder at the simple jumble of this motherless world,
look for clues that some gumpopping teenage girl
now wears my face. Full of breast milk and finger songs,
I stumble the street staring at other children,
gulping my dose of their giggles,
cursing the trees for their teeth.

The Architect

for LITTLE RICHARD

Turning a timed pout toward the camera,
he pulls himself to full swell and says,
"*I* am the architect of rock and roll!"

The politically correct black host
giggles uncomfortably and begins, "You are the architect . . . ?"
"*I said I am the,* wait a minute, is this mike on, *I said
I am the architect of rock and roll!!!*
Now that Elvis,
he was a pretty boy,
and he sure could sing,
and Lord knows he sho nuff dead now y'all,
but he wouldn't have been him
if it wasn't for me.
I took long sounds like *eeee* and *oooo* and *ahhh*
and had them white kids rubbing up 'gainst each other
making them sparks
that made them fires
their mamas and daddies couldn't put out.
Now that Jerry Lee Lewis—shame on that boy
marrying that baby and calling it love—now I might
surrender to a little peach makeup now and then
and outline my big eyes in black,
but I ain't into sinning with no babies.

Yeah, I'm hip to what he could do with a piano,
make those keys rise up and dance on their own,
but you couldn't call what come out of that boy's throat singing;
you'd think somebody was choking that boy.
Now the key to it—
you know, did I tell you, wait a minute now,
did I tell you *I'm* the architect of rock and roll?
Now the key to it is the squeal,
my eyes wide open and gleaming like a crazy colored boy,
white folks see that one time and it scares 'em—
they trip all over each other running out to buy the record.

Now I ain't never been what you'd call *sexy,*
at least not in the normal way,
but I been burning the kinks outta this hair ever since I could,
and I can still turn the eyes
of some young boy
aching to hook on to a legend.
If I do say so *my*self,
I still got my hips,
still got that smooth line
straight down to the point in my patent leathers,
still turn some eyes now and then.

But when I'm up on stage
I sit my pretty ass right down behind that piano.
Chuck Berry, that ol' fool, kicking and duckwalking,
he know he too old for that teenage mess,
and makin' them dirty movies on the side.
You know, I'm 'bout the only one who stayed pure;

partial as I am to a little *eyeliner* now and then,
I done kept clean.

Ain't fathered but two babies in this life;
named one Rock 'n' and the other one Roll,
that's them in your ear.

Now you can call me sissy,
but I'm the builder,
the breath,
the man you wants to pretend you was.
Bee bop a loo bop a bop bam boom, baby,
I'm the architect—
And the building
ain't finished
yet."

Sweet Daddy

62. You would have been 62.
I would have given you a Roosevelt Road kinda time,
an all-night jam in a twine-time joint,
where you could have taken over the mike
and crooned a couple.

The place be all blue light
and JB air
and big-legged women
giggling at the way
you spit tobacco into the sound system,
showing up some dime-store howler
with his pink car
pulled right up to the door outside.

You would have been 62.
And the smoke would have bounced
right off the top of your head,
like good preachin'.
I can see you now,
twirling those thin hips,
growling 'bout if it wasn't for bad luck
you wouldn't have no luck at all.
I said,
wasn't for bad luck,
no luck at all.

Nobody ever accused you
of walking the paradise line.
You could suck Luckies
and line your mind with rubbing alcohol
if that's what the night called for,
but Lord, you could cry foul
while B.B. growled Lucille from the jukebox,
you could dance like killing roaches
and kiss those downsouth ladies
on fatback mouths. "*Ooooweee*", they'd say,
"that sweet man *sho'* knows how deep my well goes."
And I bet you did, daddy,
I bet you did.

Buy hey, here's to just another number—
to a man who wrote poems on the back
of cocktail napkins and brought them home
to his daughter who'd written her rhymes
under the cover of blankets.
Here's to a strain on the caseload.
Here's to the fat bullet
that left its warm chamber
to find you.
Here's to the miracles
that spilled from your head
and melted into the air
like jazz.

The carpet had to be destroyed.
And your collected works
on aging, yellowed twists of napkin

can't bring you back.
B.B. wail and blue Lucille
can't bring you back.
A daughter who grew to write screams
can't bring you back.

But a room
just like this one,
which suddenly seems to fill
with the dread odors of whiskey and smoke,
can bring you here
as close as my breathing.

But the moment is hollow.
It stinks.
It stinks sweet.

Instructions to a Poet Who Suspects His Own Mediocrity

Do not open your vein until the reading begins.
Quick. Get happy.
Turn your eyes toward something brilliant,
toward someone you can soak in,
someone who glows.
Cough politely and smile.
Create an impossible laughter.
Chuckle at your own metaphors.
Force-feed them flowers.
Quick. Reach for delirium.
Rub your poem until it grins, until it wiggles.
Shake the sad curves from your fingers,
then emote until your open places seal and scar.
Laugh aloud now. Throw your head back,
spit out remarkable words
and dare anyone to decipher them.
Fling your tangled odes at their faces.
Make them rise to their feet and sway
until the room grows too large,
until they clap crazy,
carried away like the 4th of July,
until they realize all that's missing
are the fireworks
and the sharp, sad smell that always follows.

Always in the Head

for DAMON, MESFEN
and all my young black brothers

"I seen it lots of times, I seen it, just from being
on the street when something was going down;
I seen kids get killed, a few, my buddy Jules
got bucked, this gang he was down with, I mean he
wasn't even down with them when they started
beefin' with this other gang, but one day, it was hot,
I remember it was real hot, somebody called Jules
and he opened the window and looked out and
they got him in the head; you know all the
time now you got to get 'em in the head,
gotta bust that brain, man, don't shoot
'em in the head most likely they won't die,
and if they don't die you might as well kill
yourself cause soon as they can stand up
they be stalkin' you big time, man, might as well
blow yourself away. Gotta bust that brain, man.
But you know what was funny, even the folks
Jules was down with didn't know who smoked him
cause they was beefin' with so many other gangs,
and then there was Billy, they jacked him big time,
took him out just for talkin' shit, acting like he was
down with brothers who didn't even know his ass,
cockin' them colors wrong, and I'm sorry for laughin',
I know the shit ain't funny, but I was still looking to
see my boys hangin' in the hood, jivin' and scopin'

the bitches, but then I saw them at the wake, laid out
man, lyin' stiff, skin two colors too light, wearin' wigs
to hold their heads on and they mamas clawin' at them
and screamin' out their heads for Jesus, then I knew
Jules and Billy wouldn't be hangin' no more, but after
awhile you just deal with dyin', you get cold with it.
It's like, 'Yo man, somebody got their cap peeled last night,
you know who it was? Man, not him man, that's foul,
he was down, man, you goin' to the wake? No man,
can't make it, got a game, gotta kick some ass on the court.'
You just take in the word, you know, about somebody dyin'
and you deal with it, can't let it twist you round and
mess your head up cause then you let your guard down
and like I said before then you might as well kill yourself.
Me? I ain't sweatin' bout dyin'. I'm kickin' the right colors,
got my brim twisted proper. Sometimes it's even fun
hangin' out at places most people are scared of,
like down at Dudley late at night, the game is not
knowin' if you gon be there when somethin' goes down
and somethin' always does. Somebody gets bucked and
hits the street and some folks will say, 'Oh man, that's
too bad,' but almost everyone else will say, 'Did you see
that guy get shot? That was live, man. Did you see how
he ran, how he fell, how he screamed like a girl?
They got him in the head, man, they *busted* that brain,
It was like the movies, man. He screamed like a fuckin' girl.' "

Tuesday, wind shakes the windows. No one is outside,
at least not that I can see, and my son pulls on
a second sweatshirt, a bulky goosedown coat. He is 15,

a year younger than Jules, a year older than the child
who saw Jules open the window
to answer to his name, to let in some air.

There are times I hate being a reporter.
I am afraid of the stories. The voices are too real,
the colors too strong.
I rewind the tape, open another computer file,
hear my son yell goodbye and slam the door
on his way out. I run to the window.
Yes, his head is covered.

Medusa

Poseidon was easier than most.
He calls himself a god,
but he fell beneath my fingers
with more shaking than any mortal.
He wept when my robe fell from my shoulders.

I made him bend his back for me,
listened to his screams break like waves.
We defiled that temple the way it should be defiled,
screaming and bucking our way from corner to corner.
The bitch goddess probably got a real kick out of that.
I'm sure I'll be hearing from her.

She'll give me nightmares for a week or so;
that I can handle.
Or she'll turn the water in my well into blood;
I'll scream when I see it,
and that will be that.
Maybe my first child
will be born with the head of a fish.
I'm not even sure it was worth it,
Poseidon pounding away at me, a madman,
losing his immortal mind
because of the way my copper skin swells in moonlight.

Now my arms smoke and itch.
Hard scales cover my wrists like armor.

C'mon Athena, he was only another lay,
and not a particularly good one at that,
even though he can spit steam from his fingers.
Won't touch him again. Promise.
And we didn't mean to drop to our knees
in your temple,
but our bodies were so hot and misaligned.
It's not every day a gal gets to sample a god,
you know that. Why are you being so rough on me?

I feel my eyes twisting,
the lids crusting over and boiling,
the pupils glowing red with heat.
Athena, woman to woman,
could you have resisted him?
Would you have been able to wait
for the proper place, the right moment,
to jump those immortal bones?

Now my feet are tangled with hair,
my ears are gone. My back is curving
and my lips have grown numb.
My garden boy just shattered at my feet.

Dammit, Athena,
take away my father's gold.
Send me away to live with lepers.
Give me a pimple or two.
But my face. To have men never again

be able to gaze at my face,
growing stupid in anticipation
of that first touch,
how can any woman live like that?
How will I be able
to watch their warm bodies turn to rock
when their only sin was desiring me?

All they want is to see me sweat.
They only want to touch my face
and run their fingers through my . . .

my hair

is it moving?

After Green Mill, March 1988

I was intrigued by your position papers
presented over drinks that numbed our tongues
and whistled steam. Your variation on the
age-old theme of opposites attract
went on possibly a sunset too long
and was noticeably thick on violin.

And what did we conclude?
You ache for a spark. I lock onto heat sources.
You are wary of building. I was born of bricks.
Vivaldi's *Four Seasons*? Motown's Four Tops.
You spout witticisms in battered French,
share pieces of meat with shards of onion.
Like most Negroes of your station, you know
cheese well, boast of visiting the motherland.

No, the chance that I will fall
in love with you no longer exists.
It is a fortunate loss of option, the early death
of a rather indistinct possibility,
the end before beginning, a rotten novel.
It's just as well. In the mornings, I hate your smell.

But what will you do with the pieces of me,
those sharp, insistent slivers,
that probe deeper and deeper each time

you draw that shaky breath the way you do,
searching for the one cliché I haven't heard?

And how will you translate that rumble when
my tongue touches your ass? I would not be
you for anything just then. And I wouldn't
fret your seduction any longer.
It is now simply a matter of rhyming words.
There is nothing wrong, I've heard,
with slipping on a darker skin when occasion warrants
or the reading aloud of poems meant for others.

Climbing to Erice

SICILY, 1986

This high above the sea, my startled heart
rattles in its cage. Each breath struggles
through its natural pull, needles challenging stone.

So I lock in on the crooked melody of the Volvo's rasping engine,
wondering why human parts grow dumb
when threatened with the specter of heaven,
while cogs, wheels and motors push on.
Denied the sweet surety of oxygen, my rhythm goes crazy.
Our speed whacks away precious bits of the narrowing road,
each tight curve unveiling hillside cottages,
sloped and scrambled as first arithmetic,
or the sudden Mediterranean,
all overwrought glint and ripple
like a ragged, long discarded shred of silk.

The man behind the wheel,
pointing the car's silver teeth toward heaven,
knows that water and its cool runnings
have never comforted me. I am clearly unnerved
by this flopped equation of thin air and thick color,
but still he says, "Higher."

I bury my fright in his grip on the wheel,
pray in my fashion,

wonder if some deity's merciful hand
will part the clouds to lift me away.
Erice, its plumage veiled by mist,
is a weary bird caged by this height,
a city high enough to know hurt.
Stuffed with silvery fish and sweet cheese,
she rumbles along with our struggle,
sleeps when she can.

Tonight, the man seduced by the thin arms of this city
will hold a pearl onion between two fingers,
slip it smoothly into my mouth,
whisper, "bella negri" as if they were words *he* discovered.
"You will long for nothing more than this," he'll tell me,
bracing my body against the chilled torso of an olive tree.

We spend the night on this mountain, drugged by the click
in our breathing, imagining ourselves gentle Joves,
benevolent rulers of the serenity below us.
Looking down on the cool patchwork of ordered lives,
he points a finger,
blesses one house with a child.
With a wave of my hand,
I craft a fisherman's final dream.

Tiring of fate, we push down the seats of the Volvo
and sleep to the steady hum of this breathless heaven,
the moon rising like stones in our throats.
Is it too much to ask? I want this night to live in my bones.
I want nothing anchored or earthbound. Ever.

Nickel Wine and Deep Kisses

CABRINI GREEN HOUSING PROJECT,
CHICAGO, 1982

"Hey, miz lady . . . bring your fine ass over here and talk to
   me . . ."

I never assumed it a casual flirtation.
I knew you were as serious as the sidewalk
you stood on, from your studiously gaping gym shoes
to the Adidas symbol shaved carefully into the back
of your hair. I knew you hissed, *"Hey, miz lady . . ."*
exactly the way you meant to,
with promises of nickel wine and deep kisses
in a moonwashed Cabrini corner.
Even the industrious rumble of Division St. traffic
couldn't drown out the answer to my headache
screaming from the front of your jeans.

Sheathed in wool and oxford, briefcased and correct,
I scurried past your steamy threat
with just a bit of inherited shimmy,
and you saw it in me,
the bottom line I've tried for so long to hide.
Hey, I've done my bit for the underclass,
just don't intrude,
don't invade,
don't insist,

don't push me,
don't flick that switch,
don't make me mingle.

But behind midnight black shades,
your lizard-lidded eyes
cupped the cheeks of my ass and held on.
You were clearly not considering
the possibility of being turned down,
just wondering whether to turn me on
or turn me out.

Bad Cabrini baby, I've been warned about you.
In your eyes, I'd be less than nothing,
a willing receptacle for your accumulated heat.
I'd be your downtown woman,
and each time you sensed rebellion
you'd grab at my chest
through my oh-so-correct clothing
or appeal to my bragged-about liberal sensibilities.

You'd make me climb piss-slick stairs
to the box you lived in
and you'd pin me to a roach-eaten mattress,
tearing away at my nine-to-five with your teeth,
fucking away at my uptown bourgeoise
at
ti
tude.
You'd play your role of underprivilege to the hilt,
wallowing in your furious clouds of reefer and wine,

daring me to once again
draw that socially acceptable line between us.

And I'd go on living my two lives,
playing Peter to your Jesus,
lying to my mother about the bright bruises
on my body,
denying your smell on my skin
three different times
to three different people.
And you'd always be waiting for me
at the entrance from one world to the other.

"Hey miz lady, come on back. Let's spend some time."
Harmless enough, so I let loose my smile
and hurry away. You listen to my heels apologize.
Cause you know that your real meaning
will cling like brown to my skin all day:

"Come back here, bitch.
I'll eat you alive."

Pretending Sleep

again, my son is pretending sleep.
but there is a bristling in the room's air,
the faint smell of fire where his feet have touched.
doors are busily left unlatched, cars and
pennies tossed about like a poet's commas. his lie

is further unfurled by his scat song breathing
and the clink of lashes against his skin.

in this room, smells mingle like drunken dancers.
last week's scientific endeavor has flopped, and now
fizzles vindictively in a corner. raspberry gum stabilizes
a bridge of toothpicks. brittle corners of bread have been
shot from rifles, and GI Joe, caught once again behind
enemy lines, was tortured for hours in a cup of maple syrup.

i could sit here for hours,
and sometimes do, watching streetlights click
their changes in the kinks of his hair,
fingering the worried edges of first love letters,
discovering failed French tests crammed into pockets,
watching his body ache with deliberate stillness,
his eyes tracing my travels beneath trembling lids.

i never know what i'm waiting for until i hear it.
only the stars and i are witness

as the night overwhelms and with one struggling
sigh he moves out of this quiet room,
beyond his knowing,
beyond deception,
beyond any mother.

Your Man

Your man walks in on wishbone legs,
smelling like hot sauce and black pepper,
bringing me blues bound up like roses
every Thursday night 'bout this time.

Your man brings me sweet bread and fried corn,
feeds me like an animal from his fingers,
tames me like an animal with his hips.
Your man comes in sweatin' his blue collar
and singin' those lies, those washaway dreams.

I wait for his mouth, the mercy circle.
I wait for his mouth. The mercy circle.
He neatly arranges the gasping of my skin,
leaves me gentle and crazed on a trembling bed.

Your man's lovin' leaves marks like drumbeats,
disturbances on brown skin stretched across a circle of bone.
I carved his coming out of a mojo moonlight,
out of what you told me
about the voodoo in his fingers.

He says, *"Bitch, lie still,"* and I do, I do.
He says, *"Squeeze harder,"* and I want to.
Your man hurls light against my skin
and forgets your name when that's what I need.

Yeah. Your man is your man,
but he visits me sometimes,
he rocks the house sometimes,
he shakes it up sometimes,
he makes it right. All the time.
Sometimes.

Skinhead

They call me skinhead, and I got my own beauty.
It is knife-scrawled across my back in sore, jagged letters,
it's in the way my eyes snap away from the obvious.
I sit in my dim matchbox,
on the edge of a bed tousled with my ragged smell,
slide razors across my hair,
count how many ways
I can bring blood closer to the surface of my skin.
These are the duties of the righteous,
the ways of the anointed.

The face that moves in my mirror is huge and pockmarked,
scraped pink and brilliant, apple-cheeked,
I am filled with my own spit.
Two years ago, a machine that slices leather
sucked in my hand and held it,
whacking off three fingers at the root.
I didn't feel nothing till I looked down
and saw one of them on the floor
next to my boot heel,
and I ain't worked since then.

I sit here and watch niggers take over my TV set,
walking like kings up and down the sidewalks in my head,
walking like their fat black mamas *named* them freedom.
My shoulders tell me that ain't right.

So I move out into the sun
where my beauty makes them lower their heads,
or into the night
with a lead pipe up my sleeve,
a razor tucked in my boot.
I was born to make things right.

It's easy now to move my big body into shadows,
to move from a place where there was nothing
into the stark circle of a streetlight,
the pipe raised up high over my head.
It's a kick to watch their eyes get big,
round and gleaming like cartoon jungle boys,
right in that second when they know
the pipe's gonna come down, and I got this thing
I like to say, listen to this, I like to say
"Hey, nigger, Abe Lincoln's been dead a long time."

I get hard listening to their skin burst.
I was born to make things right.

Then this newspaper guy comes around,
seems I was a little sloppy kicking some fag's ass
and he opened his hole and screamed about it.
This reporter finds me curled up in my bed,
those TV flashes licking my face clean.
Same ol' shit.
Ain't got no job, the coloreds and spics got 'em all.
Why ain't I working? Look at my hand, asshole.
No, I ain't part of no organized group,

I'm just a white boy who loves his race,
fighting for a pure country.
Sometimes it's just me. Sometimes three. Sometimes 30.
AIDS will take care of the faggots,
then it's gon be white on black in the streets.
Then there'll be three million.
I tell him that.

So he writes it up
and I come off looking like some kind of freak,
like I'm Hitler himself. I ain't that lucky,
but I got my own beauty.
It is in my steel-toed boots,
in the hard corners of my shaved head.

I look in the mirror and hold up my mangled hand,
only the baby finger left, sticking straight up,
I know its the wrong goddamned finger,
but fuck you all anyway.
I'm riding the top rung of the perfect race,
my face scraped pink and brilliant.
I'm your baby, America, your boy,
drunk on my own spit, I am goddamned fuckin' beautiful.

And I was born

and raised

right here.

Big Towns, Big Talk

My mama done told me, when I was in pigtails,
my mama done told me, "Hon,
I been in some big towns . . ."
—"Blues in the Night"

I heard me some big talk,
from big men and mama's boys,
from rednecks, bluebloods and brownnoses,
talk round and plump with Mississippi juice,
talk wiry and hot with West Coast snarl,
positive talk with double negatives,
talk as tall as cities,
as flat and dry and joyless
as Iowa cornfields,
talk I couldn't bear to witness,
the talk my daddy talked
that made my mama walk,
talk that heated my hips
and curled my hair,
talk that made me paint my nails,
talk saying *sit yo' fast brown self down*
and listen to the sugar pouring out
this man's mouth, talk so sweet
it made my teeth hurt.
I heard lies so good made me want
to lie down and roll around in 'em.
I heard me some big talk
from fry cooks in Chi-Town,

Memphis bus drivers,
hustlers in the Motor City,
big men in D.C.,
undertakers in Dallas,
pimps in Vegas,
and poets in Boston.
I heard words that shoulda been songs,
words that shoulda been warnings,
words with big feet for dancing.
I heard big talk
talk with the vowels stretched long
and the nouns long gone,
I heard
I love you,
each word separate and sore
like a mistake in the mouth,
mumbled by an Alabama pump jockey
with his yellowed teeth
scraping the side of my face.

I heard it hissed
by one of them pretty Italian boys
who didn't know
where one word ended
and the next one began.
I heard it sung in my ear, off key and
with no traces at all of soul
by a man who danced closer to me
than my skin
and made me burn.

These boys own all the bad words,
"I love you" being just three of them,
and by no means the worst.

I've danced the wide words of jazzmen,
their music rumbling
through the splintered reed my body is,
and I have struggled for breath
beneath the word "stay,"
whispered by men bluer than black,
playing my bones like the ivory keys,
lit cigarettes like fuses at their lips.

My mama done told me,
a man's gonna big talk
and give you the sweet eye.

I have rocked these big men to sleeping,
and I have been vessel for that big talk,
I have been feast for that sweet eye.

In every corner of this big town
there's a man whose spine rattles
when I whip the hem of my purple dress
against his knees.
There's always a man
who suddenly discovers
that red whiskey won't work this time,

won't loose his tongue,
that this fever
called long brown woman
can make his pretty lips
move around nothing
and that the words I give him—
the ones *I* give him—
are the only ones he has.

III.

THE WORD

The Word

It was funny the way the word flew out of my mouth without stopping. Haven't you ever flashed on something a beat before it happens, with plenty of time to consider and reverse and rearrange, but instead you just sit by like a dumb animal while it happens?

You see the brick in front of your left foot in time to stop and you clench your teeth and get ready to trip and fall instead of swerving one way or the other. You're about to add sugar to a recipe and pick up the salt instead and pour and pour even as you're checking out that perky bitch with the umbrella on the side of the box. You feel your mouth ready to say "nah" to your mother when all of your life you'd said "No, maam" and you had to live through that moment when her eyes got all wide just before she picked up a shoe or a strap or a douche bag to beat you to within an inch of your miserable little life.

So the word, which I felt taking shape behind my teeth and snuggling there for a moment, flew out of my mouth and didn't stop. The sound hit the air with a smack. It only felt sour for a moment, then it felt okay. It didn't feel *right*, but it felt okay.

We're almost never right about stuff before we've done it. We think it's one way, then we do it for the first time and find out it's something else. I always thought the mouths of pale boys would taste like cotton, which was the sheerest, most shapeless thing I could think of. I thought kissing a woman would be like kissing a mirror. I thought I'd look stupid doing the nasty dances. I thought I could never swallow an oyster or a chocolate-drenched grasshopper or a chunk of octopus or a fish's eye.

But I did all those things, and I was wrong about them. I'd do most of them again.

So the word flew out, and I didn't get punished or yelled at or slapped. In fact, no one noticed or even looked at me curiously. The world kept spinning merrily along and the day moved and pretty soon the sun became a smear and the night dropped *boom* and soon it was the next day and I wondered if I could say the word again. I certainly didn't feel any different.

When you got laid for the first time, didn't you expect that the next day there would be the slightest faint pink aura outlining your invaded body, and that everyone would know but it would be alright because everyone did it, except maybe your grandparents? Didn't you expect to feel different? Didn't you expect your walk to change, your curves to turn into angles, your appetite to never slow down again, didn't you expect to have more pubic hair? When you got laid for the first time, didn't you expect flowers every day, late steamy phone calls, a pet name like Coco? Didn't you expect murmurs and Motown and the most marvelous marriage? Didn't you expect to feel hot down there forever?

I expected to feel different when I said the word. I wanted it to mean something, that I could say the word without flinching or blinking or being yelled at or punished. But it wound up that the word didn't mean anything to anybody anymore. So it just flew out of my mouth without stopping and I said it. I said it, and that was all.

We're almost never right about stuff before we've done it. We think it's one way, then we do it for the first time and find out it's something else altogether. Like pale boys' mouths not tasting like cotton and an oyster sliding down my throat. I kissed a pale boy for the first time while we were having dinner, marveling at the different tastes coming from his throat, and he moved an oyster hidden in his cheek gently into my mouth and it moved down easy, the same way singing moves up. He'd been trying to get me to try oysters all night and I wouldn't. It was one of those beautiful, warm moments that are only beautiful and warm because you're young and haven't done a lot of things. You pick flowers and smell them on your fingers for days. You say things like, "I'll never leave you."

So I said the word and I didn't feel any different. Here was a word that shaped me, made me cry, made me spit and sputter and scream, made me walk for years like a shadow through the city, with my eyes pointed down and my breathing as quiet as I could make it. Here was the last word my great-grandfather heard before he died, and here I said it and I just said it, that's all.

I said the word to a friend who says the word all the time. He said the word so much that it was like *chair* or *sink* or *trenchcoat,* like the breath you take during a pause in conversation, like he couldn't stand to feel the word on his tongue for too long and had to get it out.

So when I said the word, why should it mean anything to him? The first time I heard the word, the first time it became part of what I am, it hit me.

I was what you call a disadvantaged kid, which is to say I lived on the west side of Chicago with roaches and canned goods and parents who were factory workers. But I was good in school because I liked words, and I was picked to be part of a program that sent city kids to the country but left the country kids where they were. (I thought it would be funny to send one of those countryfied kids to live with me, my mama and daddy, and the roaches who fell from the ceiling into our faces when we were sleeping at night.) But I wound up in a place called Stockton, Ill. with a redheaded family who drank warm, funny-smelling milk straight from the cow. Sometimes I even saw blood in it.

Anyway, this was a pretty decent family. I guess they had to be decent, or crazy, in Stockton to take a little colored girl into their home, and since there wasn't much to do but swing and play ball and get up at 5 A.M. in the fucking morning for breakfast, the family—a mom and pop and two kids—tried their best to entertain me, and part of entertaining me meant taking me to the K-Mart in Freeport. They talked about it for days like we were going to a goddamned amusement park or something. I tried my best to act like I was excited, but I'd been to K-Marts before and I'd never stayed up all night in anticipation.

In this K-Mart folks looked at me like I was naked. I'll bet you never had that sensation of being naked in a place where everyone else was wearing clothes. Everyone had hard red faces, looking at me like how dare I come into that place naked and black and ashy, and I kept looking down like a fool even though I knew I'd dressed that morning in red pants and a white shirt and my new gym shoes. I thought I looked pretty, at least every single member of the redheaded family had told me I did, and now everybody was looking at me with their faces all scrunched up like mine was when I looked at my first oyster and thought about swallowing it. So I couldn't wait to get out of there, not just out of that riveting K-Mart but out of that hick town, out of the lives of the redheaded family and into the hard edges of the city where when someone looked at me crazy I'd look back at them at the same way.

Finally we were in the checkout line, and the redheaded family had treated me to a pair of gold earrings that were turning green even before the cashier had rung them up. A little mop-haired kid in front of us sat in the baby seat of a cart with an identical mop-haired mother paying for her stuff, which seemed to be mostly candy, diapers, and laxative.

The kid's voice was sweet and I saw the word coming, saw something bad in the kid's eyes, but I couldn't stop her and she wasn't about to stop.

"Look, mama. A nigger."

Nigger. The word flew out without stopping. I saw the word coming, the little mop-haired kid and her mop-haired mother felt the word coming, the redheaded family felt the word coming, but there we were, a whole shitload of dumb animals, watching it happen. The mop-haired mother put her hand hard over the child's mouth, as if she could trap the word after the fact, but it was out in the air for everyone to feel. It hung there a moment before it entered me, where it spread like piss spreads through a diaper, warm and sticky and smelly and poison if you let it sit too long. My body felt heavier.

For years, the word was my secret. I heard it become a curse, then a sneer, then a joke, then just another part of talking. Now it's like saying *Buddy* or *Joe* or *Tyrone* like in "Nigger, you must be joking," or "Nigger, if you don't get out of my face, you better," but sometimes—especially when it comes out between clenched teeth—the word means exactly what it means.

So the first time I said the word, I just said it. I waited for it to mean something, but my friend had said something funny and I rolled my eyes and said *"Nigga, please."* The word just came out of my mouth without stopping. It didn't mean anything, anything at all. It snuggled behind my teeth for a second, but when it began to fly it didn't stop.

The word came out of me fast, the same way it entered me at that K-Mart in Freeport, hard and ugly and without thinking. My friend laughed. My mouth was sour for a moment. Just for a moment, and then it was gone.

IV.

NOBODY'S
BLUES
BUT MINE

In the Ultimate Blues Bar

men sip their bitter cocktails,
slide damp dollars across the bar,
and wheeze in rhythm,
resenting the relentless thump
of their late-night hearts.
They speak fondly of natural disasters,
predict how the missing child
will be found naked beneath a blanket of dead leaves.

Someone pops a quarter in the jukebox,
and feet tap to the dirge of downbeats,
the been-done-wrong grunts
that slug through the blood like a blind fighter.

When a woman rips a man open,
this is where he comes to bleed.

I shoulda known the bitch was no good,
a truck driver screams from his corner table,
I shoulda seent she was what she was.
The circus lights from the jukebox
break across his face,
fill his toothless mouth with color
as he screams the name *Janet!*,
as he curses it up and down the greasy walls,
drags it in the muck on the floor in front of his friends.

He pulls the name back up on the table
and he tries to slice his wrists with it,
he holds the name up against his skull
and waits for it to scatter his brains,
he swallows it
and sits death still
so the poison can creep into his blood.

He takes the name *Janet!*
and he rocks the room with it,
I shoulda seent she was no good for me,
I shoulda listened to my friends,
I shoulda looked deep into her smokey black eyes
and walked out on what they told me,
and and dammit dammit *Janet!* and screaming
the name over and over
like he's purging his belly of bad whiskey,
he staggers to the jukebox
and plays another long slow song
by a blind black man.

Tonight he's got that run
from Moline to Macon,
and Janet will sleep curled in a bigger bed,
a deep purple gash over her eye,
another man on her mind.

Bless them.
Bless them as they weep on their own sagging shoulders,
rolling the soft syllables of love around in their mouths.

Bless them
as they fill the bartender's ear
with blues he pretends he's never heard,
as he nods patiently to every twist of their gut,
bless them
as even the shot glasses
take on the curves of women.

Bless them
as the barkeep closes shop
and our boys link wobbly arms
and croon their blues to an amused moon
who bends their hearts
until she realizes
that only a woman
has the balls
to break them.

The Spinning Gone

For the friends and families of the 27 people
killed in Killeen, Texas, when George
Hennard drove his pickup truck through
the window of a crowded restaurant, then
opened fire before taking his own life.

Imagine the way the head spins
after a night of drinking liquor so raw and startling
it snarls and snaps, caged in the throat.
Imagine no food and gulping this stuff like water
and imagine the way the head must feel afterwards,
spinning without core,
thrown skyward from the fingers of a strong hand.
And imagine
that this spinning goes on all the time,
that it never stops,
even as the head swells
and the neck bends and weakens
beneath the whirling. Imagine this all the time.
Imagine never sleeping, the solid white pain
of words rotting in the mouth,
the stomach always choking toward nothing.

A smooth hard stone lodged beneath the eyelid.

A blunt dirty nail bursting
through the thin pink skin at the bottom of the foot.

A sleek and flashing razor
shoved into and through the fingertip.

And the spinning.
Imagine all of that all of the time.

When you slam your eyes shut against this thinking,
I am what you will see.
Open those eyes as wide as a screaming mouth
and you will know me,
you will see me.
There's this spinning all the time.

The Texas sun is a woman,
a ball buster, a real uncompromising bitch.
She dances with me sometimes.
I hold her tight to stop the spinning,
and she whispers into my blistered ear:
"Imagine having no head at all," she says.
Imagine the spinning gone."

The key feels as heavy as the earth in my hand.
The engine turns and turns,
spins, and I imagine the spinning gone.

The sun won't leave me alone.
"*Drive*," the bitch says, and I do.
She laughs and drapes herself
like a teasing lover across the glass
so that I no longer see the people inside.

Say, Can You See

A homeless man in New York's Tompkins
Square Park scrambles to his feet as the
"Star-Spangled Banner" blares from a
transistor radio.

Oh say, we've seen too much.
"The Star-Spangled Banner" pushes
like a cough through America's mouth
and the twilight's last gleaming is exactly that,
a sickly final flash above our heads
as we ride unsuspecting in the bellies of old trains,
plop to our knees in churches
to embrace truths that disgust us,
as we tumble beneath tangled sheets
judging and savoring the skin of lovers,
silently comparing their delinquencies to our own.

What so proudly we wail the anthems of AM radio,
electrified rhythms siphoned from black boys
on the streets of Roxbury, what so proudly we wail
those instant grade school stanzas praising wheatfields
we have never seen, what so proudly we wail
each precise and stagnant chant we have been taught,
pledging allegiance with misty eyes,
hands slapped over our blubbering hearts,
what so proudly we fail to wail our frantic
verses of "no, dammit, no more," what so proudly

we fail to hear it, the song we really need to sing,
great gulping syllables, off–target, off–key,
loud enough to shake the dust off cities,
a song cluttered with impossible chords and sour obscenities,
brash and crazy beautiful in the air,
but this is not the song that snakes through us
as our hungry mouths move once again into praise mode
and how
wonderfully that thin, tinny melody is pulled
through the air, and the man wears his
body on his back, who carries his clothes in his hair,
feels his switch flipped and god bless this america
as it seems he is standing forever, up, up.

Tabloid Headline: Haunted Elvis Lamp Sings Burning Love

She found no comfort in her garden, where her
hands just grew sticky and sore with the questions
flowers leave behind. But she sat there for hours,
feeling a vengeful morning sun bite into her shoulders
and poking at fat, sluggish worms with her toes.
She wondered why her mouth felt so wrong around prayers.

She shuffled through her stock phrases:
Nothing works anymore. Life's a bitch.
Each day's a blessing. Where there's a will—

ahunka, hunka.

That tiny insanity drifted fitfully on the wind
from the farthest corner of her house,
from the room where she'd locked her struggles—
the headless Barbie dolls
balanced on their pert toes and torpedo breasts,
roses dried and pressed into solemn little books,
crinkled dresses stiff with dancing,
breathless letters in her own handwriting
signed by people she loved.

ahunka, hunka.

She pictured the lamp, unplugged,
no bulb at all beneath its pompadoured shade,

yet slamming bright then dark like a man's affections.
And the song, that funny song she heard bubbling from
the chipped porcelain throat, moved like a current through her hair.

As she rose to walk, dragging her feet through
tired brown blossoms, leaves and soil trickled from her arms.
Already, she knew the routine. Frail and beseeching,
she'd tremble like a sacrificial lamb in her room of yesterdays,
her eyes mean and small, locked upon the lamp. Waiting

for just one goddamn part of the world to click into place.
Waiting for a love that burns.
Still waiting for the lips to move.

Olive Oyl Talks to <u>People</u> Magazine

If you must know me, first know this:
I was born a bone child,
a bleached confusion of sticks
clattering from my mother's womb,
ribs fused gently around a sputtering heart.
No milk moved in the woman who made me,
so I lay in her thin arms
sucking the thought of the sea from her skin.

My father was a stevedore,
wrists of dust, his skinny pink neck
bulging with pull and push, heft and release.
My mother grew weak trying to love him,
searching for the rhythms of water
in the way his sour body folded around sleep,
his brusque demands for sex, more potatoes.
She sat at the window, watching *real* sailors.

He blossomed as her body cramped with me—
he was praying for a boy, muscles he could tame,
a fool who'd believe he was seaworthy.
But then I came—blanched, sickly,
slick with blood and effort,
hair as black and flat as a seal's.
He never held me,
and only touched me once,

his fingers tangling
in my sparse pubic hair,
then pulling away,
startled, disgusted, thrilled.
Perhaps he hoped I could be a man.
But he went no further
because he only *called* himself a sailor.

Early one morning as he helped a crew
unload the *windswept,* his heart splintered
and burst, his body falling only inches from
the sea he'd sworn to possess before he died.
His mouth filled with earth and chips of wood.
My mother screamed, refused food, followed.

I was left alone in the house of my birth,
a battered wooden shell ravaged
by wind and salt. My wide eyes were trained on the water line,
watching the rickety ships bob and pivot,
hearing the raw shouts, the thick voices of mariners.

I was still a stick interrupted by knees,
ending in huge feet caged in black shoes.
I pulled my hair tight
and looped a red ribbon through the floppy bun,
powdered coy circles on pale cheeks.
I stuffed napkins into the front of my dress
and pranced the shore, a sacrifice of toothpicks.
I wanted the man my father had wanted to be,
a man of the sea, drunk with horizons.
The rumbling one came first.

All sinew and teeth, his arms were tree trunks,
muscles screaming inside stiff cotton clothing.
His real name didn't matter. The men barked, "*Bluto!*,"
and the hard syllables swirled in my head.
A look from him would have curled my father,
made my mother rise and press her face against the window.
The helpless air crackled when he was in it,
sparks stinging my skin, currents bristling my hair.
Love made me dance around him, silly with want,
my hard black brogans clicking on the dock.
My wretched waltz amused, then confused him,
until he could not imagine the night without me.
Ribs tightened around my sputtering heart.

No music or tentative fingers, he took me
like a windstorm, left me rattled, sore.
His brash laughter boomed, and a crowd gathered
at my window to watch him suck
tiny red stars into the skin of my throat.

He took me propped against the wall,
pinned to the rough wooden floor,
in the chipped porcelain bathtub,
against the icebox, from the front,
from behind, with his mouth and
with his cock, veined as a horse's neck.
I wept with love, bled into his cupped hand.

When he left, I went with him,
thinner than when I began, but wanting
the sea, and that man, more than anything.

He passed me to his drooling men,
roped me to the bow,
laughed at my longing.
On faraway islands bursting
with color I could smell,
he starved me,
tied me to tree trunks,
teased my body with wild tigers.
Each night he rewarded my devotion,
biting into my skin with yellowed teeth,
another letter of his name
carved into my skinny soul.
Soon he would love me more than water.

But one raucous midnight, while I prayed
no train would come rumbling down the
tracks I was tied to, the ropes loosened
and I was swept up by arms I didn't know.
I looked up into a comical squint of eyes,
smelled the briny musk of his panting
and wondered what seas this man had seen.

If Bluto was tidal wave, Popeye was ripple.
Bald, nearly blind, bubble-cheeked, a rotting pipe
teetering on his bottom lip,
my savior.
As if I had asked to be saved.
I hated him, his giddy, toothless smile,
that stupid giggle, his bulging cartoon forearms.

When he saw my scars, he blubbered like a baby,
weeping at my histories of torn skin,
not recognizing the signposts of love.
I fell asleep counting, while his mouth
touched each one.

I had no place for him
in my crazy life, yet there he was.
When he loved me,
laying me down as if I were a rose,
my wounds found new skin.
I was too beautiful to be me.

But now my life borders on slapstick.
I walk into traps, tumble into rushing rivers,
one-eyed ogres dangle me over spitting volcanoes.

Bluto snatches me from Popeye's bed,
slams his want into me, threatens me with blades.
Popeye gobbles what he can of the earth
and risks his life to find me,
beats Bluto senseless, then it all begins again.
My body stretches between them, thinner than ever.

Popeye wants to marry me, make an honest
woman out of a hot, bony stevedore's daughter.
Bluto lights a match, holds it to my nipple.

You ask how I can love them both,
how these bones have carried them for so long.

If you must know, first know this:
I was raised by the water,
crafted by these tides,
a stick child, never wise or beautiful.
Whatever I loved loved the water first.
And I will die possessing these sailing men
who fight over my frail body,
craving my flesh,
neglecting the sea.

I Think It's That One

LOS ANGELES—People who want to claim
a body from the coroner's office will first
have to identify the corpse in a photo
lineup under guidelines established after a
woman gained custody of a body to fake
her own death certificate.

I'm here, second from the left,
one foot twisted in, pigeon-crooked,
brown-skinned, startled hair,
eyes ignorant to the surprise of flashing.
The skin of my final body,
shocked and giddy in perfect polaroid light,
is not my skin. Perhaps it is the first veneer of angels.

I came here wrong. I plopped here with
an ugly twist, no white light glimmered
the hall of my entry. I imagined
more—short welcoming toots of woodwind,
bone white dancers fragile as breath,
my ankles turning to glass.
Not this cold splintered wood,
these shocking surfaces of silver,
knives, machines, suction,
chilly fingers, obscene flashing.
Propped here beside the really dead,
puffed full and glorious with sudden light,

I wonder if I am smiling,
what they have done with my blood,
if you will scream

or if you will
keep staring at the picture,
my name asleep in your mouth,

and wait.
Wait.
While I try my best
to tremble.

Pain Passing

News item: A woman burst into a California
courtroom today and fatally shot the man
who was about to go on trial for raping her
8-year-old daughter.

At first, she tried doing what they told her to do.
She put her pain in the Lord's hands.
But the Lord hurled it right back at her,
too busy that day for her twist on sorrow.

So she prayed until her knees cramped,
she prayed, out loud and alone,
until her voice broke with praying,
she prayed over the shell
that still wore her daughter's name.

At each amen, she touched the child's
quivering cheek with the back of her hand
until the night when she tilted her face
to glare at an unseen, unfeeling savior,
and hissed, "Thanks for nothing, you son of a bitch."

It was then she realized how late it really was,
how the passage of time had shaken her senseless.

So she dressed carefully. Thick, dark fabrics,
shoes with soles of rubber. A woolen scarf
in deep hues of blue. No jewelry. A petticoat of lace.

And they led him in, unbound, uncaged,
reeking of what he had taken,
her daughter raining in his wrists,
her daughter in his shoulders,
her daughter in his hips,
her daughter in the set of his jaw,
her pleas still singing in his ears,
his eyes moving like any other eyes,
his feet
pointed forward and holding his weight
like any other feet.

And the air around him all wrong.
His smile rising up dark and slapping.
"Lord I've had my fill," she whispered,
"I'll blow this pain sky high.
I'll send it back to you in pieces."

After that, it wasn't hard. It wasn't hard at all
for her to end what he held in his eyes
with what she held
in her hands.

Stop

for RUDY LINARES,
who held a Chicago hospital staff at
gunpoint after they refused to disconnect
his 2-year-old son's life support system.

When every breath wears a number,
when every in and every out
is tugged along by machines of practical gleam,
of unerring silver,
there is very little common love can do.
It all boils down to being too big,
too stupid, too illiterate,
too clumsy, too Third World,
to understand the relentless rhythms of high tech,

but he understood
the forced drumming inside his son's chest;
he understood
its link to his own heartbeat;
he understood
only too well
the losing that never stopped.

So Rudy fought the world with his face.
He denied the fists ticking behind his eyes
and learned to pray without kneeling.

It grew harder for him to click
his John Q. Public into place;
he became one with shaking,
his dreams fashioned by fever.

In each dream, the dreaded breathing
stopped.
And flowers opened.

Every sound in the world
stopped.
And color returned to his daybreaks.

The machines groaned to a
stop.
And flesh of his flesh was lifted.

So on that morning, his sleep once again
falling prey to the whitewashed downbeats,
Rudy's flat red hands covered his face,
and he knew,
and he cried,
and he knew,
and he cried,
and he knew
that every sleeping child
wears a scream on his closed lids.

So Rudy moved close and finally listened
to what he'd always heard:

Please.

Daddy.

Make it *stop.*

Summer to Fall, Chicago

Rolling the smooth syllables *Chi–ca–go* around in our mouths,
we have forgotten that summer does not belong to us.
Halsted Street vendors shiver in sunlight that was once welcoming,
hawking their colorful plastics, dogs with batteries, fake gold
necklaces as thick as tire chains. Whining mothers in Oak Park
search polished wooden chests for sweaters and acrylic mittens,
and Uptown schoolchildren still teeter with the rhythms of jumprope.

No one wants to believe in the sharp turning of air,
the showy slashes of red edging the leaves,
taunting Polaroid portraits of June lining photo album pages.
Even the lake curls away from our city, cops an attitude,
comes back gray and moody. Few notice this early signal.

Businessmen tumble onto buses and trains with a new urgency,
their shoulders hunched, health club memberships yellowing in
their pockets. Picasso's woman surveys downtown streets,
mildly amused, tarnish eating into her outlook
as she feels the first nudges of chill in her steel bones.

As the languid season of steam ends with an orange kiss
on the spires of the city, the spoiled children
of another Chicago summer deny their goosebumps
and scramble like game-show contestants
for those last tendrils of sun, digging desperate toes
into sand that has grown too cold, chilled and defiant

in their short sleeves, their giddy summer hats.
They croon loud songs of suntans and irresponsibility,
plan doomed October cookouts in Lincoln Park
and cover their ears,
their eyes,
but not their fingers,
against the brash, seductive hiss of another season.

Chinese Cucumbers

it's 3 pm on one helluva hot day and he'd been
scouring the close cluttered streets nonstop,
forgetting lunch. it's 3 pm exactly one week
after headline screamed at him from
supermarket tabloid, CHINESE CUCUMBERS
MIRACLE CURE FOR AIDS and now right in the
middle of poking around another dusty stall,
slapping aside the maggots and fruit flies,
he realizes he doesn't even know what the damned
things look like. and once he found them, if he
ever did, what next? did he peel them,
mash them, purée them, boil them, sauté
them, or simply rub the cold, unwashed
things across David's spotted skin?
should he share them with David,
forcing the crisp slices into his lover's mouth,
send pieces to their friends, pray over
them, light them like candles, offer them
as sacrifice or simply bake them up in a nice
casserole? or maybe the cure was just in
finding them—maybe the minute one of the
tight-lipped Chinese merchants admitted
he had some of the little babies stashed in
the back, David would sit up in his hospital
bed and say hey I can breathe now. maybe
the damned things weren't salvation, maybe

they were just like the oils, the oils, those
pungent greases it took him almost a year
to find, and when he did he warmed fat drops
in his hands and rubbed them over David's
sunken balls, over the withered cock, up and
down the bony legs and between the toes. then
he turned the thin shell over, warmed the oil
in his hands again and massaged David's ass
and back and waited and waited and waited
and waited, but the damned oil just glistened
under the lamplight, and David kept on dying,
dying so loud you could hear it,
he could hear it, but he also heard NEW CURE
ON THE HORIZON, crystals, yes, hung from
the neck on pure golden chains, set at angles
in the sunlight, crystals, Oprah and Phil,
Nightline and *Current Affair* screaming it,
and he heard, he held David's cracking head in
his lap and slipped the chain down on toothpick
neck, the lavender crystal burning with bad light,
glittering against David's breastbone, shaking
with his breathing and not working, not working,
dammit not working, but pretty as hell and loud
as shit. *I am one gorgeous chunk of glass* the
crystal screamed, *but what is inside this body*
I cannot pull out, I cannot silence the clicking
and wheezing or purify the rotten blood, but
have you tried the oils? made a near-dead boy
in the south end stand up in his bed and scream
HALLELUJAH! but then again he was also on the

spiritual path, repeating one thousand times a
day *i am a good person, my body is pure, i will
not die, i am a good person, my body is pure, i
will not die,* and as he guides David through
the words, watching them move sore and hurting
through the mouth, the oil matting his hair,
the crystal on fire at his throat, choking
on the chant *i am a good person, my body is
pure, i will not die,* and tomorrow wouldn't
be nearly so hot, he'd search all damned day
if he had to, and headline screamed at him
from supermarket tabloid CHINESE CUCUMBERS
MIRACLE CURE FOR AIDS and Jesus Christ the
damned things had to be somewhere.

Drumchild

for RONALD SHANNON JACKSON

The drummer man's wooden woman, her feet bound with hemp,
balances against a cymbal stand and contemplates Boston.
He brought her from Africa, the land where drums are beaten
with bones, and has strapped her to his drum set,
facing outward, so that she can snarl at America.
No one will look into her eyes.
The red-rimmed circle in her face
growls once for the open, musicless air,
again for the pink and eager dancers,
once more for the hell of it.
Behind her, the drums heave with their
simple imprints of sun, and she wriggles
to shimmy loose her shell. He'll come soon,
she feels it, his hands crafting her pulse,
the beat in the room releasing that thick,
anxious smell. He will be the colors.
And something very much like sound will swell
in the jagged hole carved for her singing.

On the Street Where She Lives

for GLORIA LYNNE

She jumped right on that last note in "On the Street
Where You Live," and in that verb's defiant tremble
my ears lost the power to receive and translate;
I tugged, pulled, sawed at the connection but it
would not break; my eyes were locked on the thin
miracle her throat was, the one note bending,
snapping, searing the hairs on my neck, and
still that one note, the exquisite shiver of a
common word, long and relentless with
you-can-kiss-my-sequinned-black-ass bravado.
I flailed in my seat, spilled my whiskey,
and still she held it,
a cool line of *live*, a furious in-my-face *live*,
an undeniably live *live*, and me without
a stitch of armor. Long time ago, when my daddy
blew hot music into my ear, why didn't he tell me
about this? Miss Gloria, conjurer woman,
on the street where you live,
the houses sport dips in their red brick hips
and their doors are open mouths, scatting songs
threaded with sweet sin, songs daddy used to hum
to rock me to sleep. On the street where you live,
time passes in two-step with a tap
of its snakeskin clickers, the sun blazes blue
and doesn't go down till it feels like it,
the streetlights jazz through their colors

and big flashy cars bend backwards
like late-night movie dancers.

She rides that last note
in "On the Street Where You Live,"
and somehow you just know
that on the street where *she* lives
no one is ever home. They've all left
to dance like fools on the boulevard,
feeling that long slow steaming in their souls
just like I feel
right now.